D1088881

SCIENCE EXPLORER

STUDYING

SINKHOLES

Follow the Clues

by Tamra B. Orr

CHERRY LAKE PUBLISHING · ANN ARBOR, MICHIGAN

Published in the United States of America by Cherry Lake Publishing
Ann Arbor, Michigan
www.cherrylakepublishing.com

CONTENT EDITOR: Robert Wolffe, EdD, Professor of Teacher Education, Bradley University, Peoria, Illinois

PHOTO CREDITS: Cover and page 1, Courtney "Coco" Mault / tinyurl.com/owmacbn / CC-BY-2.0; page 4, © iStockphoto.com/Neonci; page 5, © Daniel Schreiber/Dreamstime.com; page 6, © AP Photo; page 7, © Imaginechina via AP Images; page 8, © AP Photo/The World-Herald, Brendan Sullivan; page 9, © Ivan Pavlov/Shutterstock.com; page 10, © oticki/Shutterstock.com; page 11, © AP Photo/San Francisco Examiner, Mike Koozmin; page 12, © Alvera/Dreamstime.com; page 13, © Neutronman/Dreamstime.com; page 15, © H.S. Photos/Alamy; page 16, © AP Photo/Marcio Jose Sanchez; page 17, © AP Photo/Arizona Department of Transportation, Kim Katchur; page 18, © Antonov Roman/Shutterstock.com; page 20, © Sumit buranarothtrakul/Shutterstock.com; page 21, © Southern Light Studios/Shutterstock.com; page 22, © Garsya/Shutterstock.com; page 24, © iStockphoto.com/asiseeit; page 25, © strelov/Shutterstock.com; page 26, © Photographerlondon/Dreamstime.com; page 27, © Rob Wilson/Shutterstock.com; page 28, © AP Photo/Jose Luis Magana; page 29, © AP Photo/Alexandre Meneghini.

LIBRARY OF CONGRESS CATALOGING-IN-PUBLICATION DATA
Orr, Tamra, author.
Studying sinkholes / by Tamra B. Orr.
pages cm. — (Science explorer)
Summary: "Follow along with this exciting story to learn all about sinkholes, from how they are formed to what problems they can cause." — Provided by publisher.
Audience: Grades 4 to 6
ISBN 978-1-63362-391-0 (lib. bdg.) — ISBN 978-1-63362-419-1 (pbk.) —
ISBN 978-1-63362-447-4 (pdf) — ISBN 978-1-63362-475-7 (ebook)
1. Sinkholes—Juvenile literature. I. Title. II. Series: Science explorer.

GB609.2.O77 2016
551.44'7—dc23   2015000531

Cherry Lake Publishing would like to acknowledge
the work of the Partnership for 21st Century Skills.
Please visit www.p21.org for more information.

Printed in the United States of America, Corporate Graphics Inc.
July 2015

TABLE OF CONTENTS

CHAPTER 1

No School Today! 4

CHAPTER 2

The Power of Water 11

CHAPTER 3

Signs and Experiments 16

CHAPTER 4

Experimenting with Erosion 21

CHAPTER 5

Time to Share 26

Glossary 30

For More Information 31

Index 32

About the Author 32

NO SCHOOL TODAY!

Science experiments can be a fun activity to do at home.

"Kobe, hurry! Our school is on the news!" Molly yelled as she burst into the garage.

As usual, Kobe was standing at his workbench, doing an experiment. He called the corner of the garage his "science lab." His workbench was covered in test tubes, a microscope, a laptop computer, and a stack of books.

He frowned. Why would Kennedy Elementary be on the news? Following his twin sister into the living room, Kobe saw his parents standing in front of the television. The news reporter said, "To recap, a

relatively large sinkhole has opened up next to Kennedy Elementary in the last few hours. Experts have been called in to analyze the situation and see what needs to be done. In the meantime, Kennedy will be closed."

"Yeah!" shouted Molly, jumping around the room. "I'm doing the 'no school' dance!"

"Dad, can we go see the sinkhole?" Kobe asked eagerly. "We were just getting ready to study those in science class, and now I can see one up close."

"Sure, we can go as soon as the experts say it is safe," Mr. Hansen said. Turning to his wife, he said, "It sure seems like there are a lot more of these sinkholes than there used to be."

"Well, this is Florida," she replied. "As if hurricanes and alligators aren't enough to deal with!"

Small sinkholes are a common sight in some places.

"I remember hearing about sinkholes in Winter Haven, Jonesville, and Spring Hill just this year," Mr. Hansen added. "Plus everyone remembers the 1981 sinkhole in Winter Park. It swallowed up 250,000 cubic yards (191,139 cubic meters) right in the middle of a neighborhood."

"That was way before I was born," Kobe said. "What happened?"

Mr. Hansen settled in on the couch, and Molly and Kobe sat down next to him. Mrs. Hansen smiled. She knew how much her husband liked to tell stories.

"It was in May," he began. "A woman heard her dog barking and looked outside to see what was happening. A crack had appeared in her yard, and it was slowly getting wider. A few hours later, one of her trees fell into the crack, roots first. It made a 'ploop' sound, according to a newspaper interview."

The 1981 sinkhole in Winter Park, Florida, caused millions of dollars of damage.

Sinkholes can be very dangerous depending on where and when they occur.

"Did she leave her house?" Molly asked.

"Not until the next day. It was a good thing she got out when she did, though. The hole just kept expanding and ended up swallowing her entire house!"

Molly gasped. "Did it stop then?"

"Not at all," Mr. Hansen continued. "Eventually it grew to 350 feet (107 m) wide and 75 feet (23 m) deep. It swallowed up a car dealership, plus two streets and an Olympic-sized pool. There were TV reporters from across the country here. Tourists traveled from everywhere to see the sinkhole. In fact," he paused and then grinned, "I am fairly sure I still have a T-shirt that says 'Sinkhole '81.'"

"How did they fix the hole?" Kobe asked.

Repairing a sinkhole can be a lot of work.

"They filled it with dirt and concrete after huge cranes pulled out the cars and house."

"Why didn't they just leave that stuff in the bottom of the hole?" Molly asked.

"Good question, Mol. What do you think?"

Molly thought for a moment and then said, "Because they could pollute the water system somehow?"

"Exactly," Mr. Hansen said. "In the past, people filled sinkholes with everything from garbage to old pieces of furniture. Then they

discovered that when it rained, the rain would filter through this trash and **contaminate** local water supplies. Anyway, after they cleared the hole, it was turned into a pond. It's called Lake Rose, after the woman who saw that crack in her yard."

"Kobe, where are you going?" Mrs. Hansen asked. Kobe was slowly walking out of the living room with a thoughtful look on his face.

"I am going to research exactly what a sinkhole is and why Florida has so many of them," he replied.

"Well, we know what he'll be doing on his day off from school," Molly said with a grin.

Some sinkholes become lakes or ponds.

WHAT IS A SINKHOLE?

Droughts can cause soil to dry out and crack.

Sinkholes are found throughout the world, including in the United States. The states most at risk are Alabama, Kentucky, Missouri, Tennessee, Pennsylvania, Texas, and Florida. Florida has more sinkholes than any other state, largely because it is made up of karst. Karst is a specific type of landscape that is formed as **limestone** and **dolostone** dissolve over time. It is known for its holes and caves.

Nature and humans both do things that increase the risk of sinkholes. Heavy rains, especially following a **drought**, can raise the risk of a sinkhole appearing. Heavy pumping of groundwater, drilling new wells, and creating artificial ponds also raise the threat of a sinkhole. Burst water mains or sewer collapses are other potential factors. This is because all of these events can cause soil and rock to erode by dissolving or just washing away.

CHAPTER 2

THE POWER OF WATER

↑ Workers use brightly colored tape to keep people away from dangerous sinkholes.

The next afternoon, Mr. Hansen made some phone calls and learned that it was safe to visit the school's sinkhole. Kobe, Molly, and Mr. Hansen piled into the car. On the way to Kennedy School, they picked up Tomas, Kobe's best friend. When they arrived, they spotted the sinkhole right away. It was in the middle of the parking lot and had been roped off. Experts surrounded the hole, taking measurements and pictures. Among them was Kobe's favorite science teacher, Mr. Jennings.

"There's Mr. Jennings! Let's go talk to him," Kobe said. The three kids ran over and began peppering the teacher with questions about the sinkhole.

"Slow down," said Mr. Jennings with a grin. "I guess our unit on sinkholes will be well timed. It's the first thing we'll study once school starts up again. I suppose we could get started a little early if you want to, though."

"First things first," Molly said. "What is a sinkhole?"

Mr. Jennings chuckled. "I guess that's a good place to start. As you know, Florida gets a lot of rain. That rain soaks into the soil and starts moving toward the limestone below. As the water runs into decaying vegetation—old plants, leaves, roots, and so on—it becomes somewhat **acidic** along the way," he explained. "This acidic water slowly dissolves

Water seeps into the ground during rainstorms.

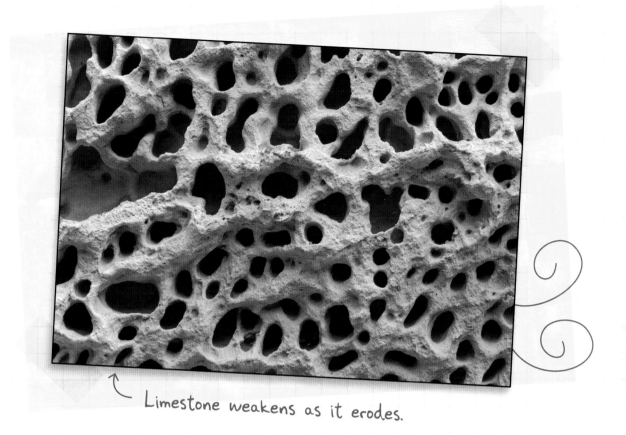

Limestone weakens as it erodes.

the limestone and washes parts of it away. Cracks known as **joints** are left in the rock. This process is called **erosion**. Over time, the joints keep getting wider. Holes called **cavities** are created. This allows even more water inside. Eventually, the rocks become unstable. On top of those holey rocks is everything that makes up the ground we're standing on—anything from asphalt and dirt to sand and clay."

"That stuff would be heavy, especially if it were wet," Tomas pointed out.

"Exactly," Mr. Jennings agreed. "That weight causes the holey limestone to collapse. Everything above the rock falls in, and you are left with a sinkhole like this one. It usually happens without any warning."

"Last night, I did some exploring online and read about **cenotes**," Kobe said.

"As usual, you've been doing some extra research," Mr. Jennings chuckled.

"Hey, aren't those sinkholes formed from underground caves?" Molly asked. "I heard something about them when we were studying the ancient Mayans a few months ago."

"Exactly," Mr. Jennings replied. "Cenotes form when the roof of an underground cave collapses. There are more than 2,000 of them in the Yucatan Peninsula of Mexico. The Mayans believed these sinkholes were a direct pathway to the underworld."

Molly frowned. "Are sinkholes dangerous?"

"It depends," said Mr. Jennings. "Most of them, like the one here, are too shallow to really hurt anyone. These are known as *cover-collapse sinkholes*. They form very quickly, usually over a matter of hours. Although most are shallow, they do have the potential to cause huge damage. The one in Winter Park in 1981 is a good example of this. Other sinkholes are called *cover-subsidence sinkholes*. They are very slow, often taking centuries to develop."

"Kids, it's time to head back home," shouted Mr. Hansen from the car.

"Hey, Kobe," Mr. Jennings said. "When you get home, check out the U.S. Geological Survey Web site. It has great information, with lots of links to explore and some experiments to try."

"That sounds awesome, Mr. Jennings," Kobe replied.

"See you when school is back in session. Oh, and when I cover this material in class, act like you haven't already heard it."

"No worries, Mr. Jennings," said Tomas with a sly grin. "We promise to pretend we're still interested."

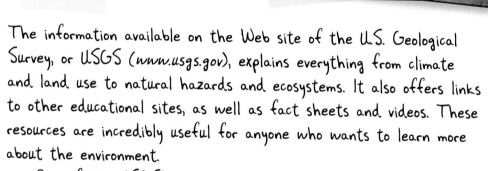

USGS scientists use special equipment to measure the rise and fall of different areas of land.

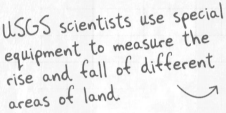

The information available on the Web site of the U.S. Geological Survey, or USGS (www.usgs.gov), explains everything from climate and land use to natural hazards and ecosystems. It also offers links to other educational sites, as well as fact sheets and videos. These resources are incredibly useful for anyone who wants to learn more about the environment.

One of the USGS's responsibilities is to create geological maps of the entire country. These maps can help people such as land planners and policy makers figure out where the risk of sinkholes is the highest. They aren't just for pinpointing sinkholes, however. USGS maps can also educate people about the risks of earthquakes, volcanoes, and landslides in different areas.

Long pipes make it easy for workers to accurately measure a sinkhole.

The next morning, Kobe, Molly, and Tomas went back to the school to learn more about the sinkhole. They watched a group of workers who were measuring the sinkhole with the help of a long pole.

"How big is it?" Tomas asked one of the workers standing nearby.

"About 3 feet (0.9 m) wide and 4 feet (1.2 m) deep," he responded. "But it is still growing."

"How will you repair it?" Molly asked.

"Mostly, we will add a lot of dirt," the man replied. "We will add layers of soil and tamp, or press, it down until we reach the top. Then the top will be repaved with asphalt. If the hole was bigger," he added, "we would start with a layer of large stones and then keep adding layers of dirt, as well as smaller stones and gravel at the top."

"Do you think the school will have another sinkhole?" Kobe asked.

"I'm not sure," the man admitted. "The **geologists** will be coming tomorrow to drill some holes into the ground for analysis. They will let us know what they find. Trying to predict a sinkhole is even harder than predicting the weather."

Some sinkholes are repaired by being filled with cement.

Soil can be very different from place to place.

"What do people watch for?" Tomas asked. "Are there any warning signs for sinkholes?"

"Actually, there are." A young woman walked over to join the group and introduced herself as Sarah Matthews, a geologist from the local college. "If an area is at risk for sinkholes, you might see cracks in the foundations of buildings or sagging fence posts. In a building, doors and windows might not close properly."

Just then, the kids heard Mr. Jennings calling out as he waved to them from across the parking lot. After thanking Ms. Matthews for the information, they ran over to see what he needed.

"Glad to see you," the teacher said. "I was hoping I could ask you three a favor. School is going to reopen tomorrow, and our first lesson is going to be about sinkholes. Because you have been spending so much time studying the hole here, I thought you might want to give a presentation to the class."

"That would be perfect," Kobe replied. "I was just thinking about the way water reaches the limestone beneath the soil, and I have a **hypothesis** I'd like to test out."

"Excellent," Mr. Jennings answered. "Perhaps you could come up with an experiment to test your hypothesis. Then you can present the findings to the class as part of the lesson."

"Gee, I can't believe Kobe wants to do an experiment," Molly said with a smirk.

"You guys can help, too," Kobe said excitedly to Molly and Tomas. "I have the perfect idea."

"I'm already looking forward to it," Mr. Jennings said. "Now I am off to look for a geologist to come in and talk to the class."

"Head over to the sinkhole and introduce yourself to Sarah Matthews," Tomas suggested. "She might be interested in helping out."

As Mr. Jennings walked off to follow Tomas's advice, Kobe unzipped his backpack and pulled out a plastic container and a small shovel. He used the tools to begin scooping up soil near the edge of the sinkhole.

"You just happened to have all of that stuff with you, Kobe?" asked Tomas with a smile.

"Of course," Kobe replied. "We need this soil for the experiment. And really, scientists should always be prepared for field—or parking lot—work!"

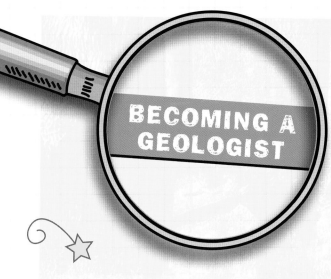

BECOMING A GEOLOGIST

There is a lot to learn by studying rocks and soil.

Geologists spend their lives studying the materials found in Earth's crust. These substances include minerals, oil, metals, and water. The information they gather helps us learn more about natural disasters such as earthquakes, landslides, floods, and volcanic eruptions.

Many geologists spend countless hours studying samples in labs. Others are found out in the field, traveling to remote locations and exploring in all kinds of environments and weather conditions. Still others work for government agencies, universities, and environmental businesses.

Some geologists may choose to focus on a certain aspect of the field. Some geology specialties include:

- Petrology: the study of rock composition
- Mineralogy: the study of minerals in rocks
- Paleontology: the study of fossils
- Marine geology: the study of coastal areas and the ocean floor

CHAPTER 4

EXPERIMENTING WITH EROSION

Household items, like empty glass jars, can be used in home experiments.

Later that afternoon, the three friends gathered around Kobe's workbench, ready to carry out the experiment. Tomas was taking notes while Molly took pictures. Kobe had spent the last hour getting materials together. So far he had three glass jars that were all the same size, a box of sugar cubes, and three plastic containers filled with soil.

"So what's the plan, Kobe?" Tomas asked.

"Well," Kobe began, "do you remember what Mr. Jennings taught us yesterday about the role rainwater plays in creating sinkholes?"

"Sure," Molly replied. "The water seeps down through the soil and wears away the stone below."

"Exactly," Kobe replied. "This made me wonder about the way water moves through the soil. The question I want to answer with this experiment is whether or not water travels at different speeds through different types of soil."

"Interesting," said Tomas. "What's your prediction?"

"I already know that soil can be made of many different things and have many different textures," Kobe explained. "So my hypothesis is that soil type will play a big role in the way rainwater reaches underground limestone."

Kobe continued, "Okay, first, we will put sugar cubes in each jar. They represent the limestone." He stacked several layers of sugar cubes in the bottom of each glass jar, making sure they were equal.

"Why sugar cubes?" Tomas asked.

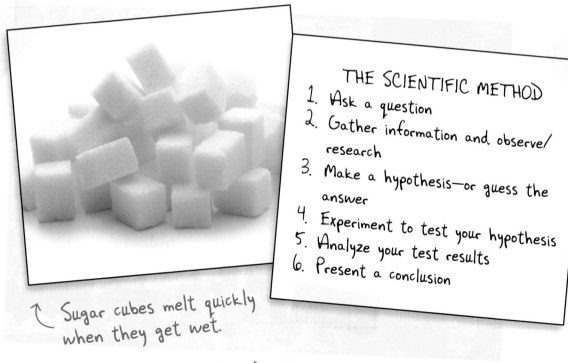

↑ Sugar cubes melt quickly when they get wet.

THE SCIENTIFIC METHOD
1. Ask a question
2. Gather information and observe/research
3. Make a hypothesis—or guess the answer
4. Experiment to test your hypothesis
5. Analyze your test results
6. Present a conclusion

"Because they will be dissolved with water like limestone is—only much faster," Kobe explained. "Next, we'll add dirt to each jar to represent **topsoil**. Before you ask, Tomas, topsoil is the upper layer of dirt where plants find the nutrients they need to grow."

"Different dirt in each jar, right?" Molly asked.

"Exactly," Kobe replied. "I have the soil I scooped up at the sinkhole site, plus some from the garden and a scoop of the sandy stuff out near the road. Let's make sure we use the same amount in each jar."

Soon, each jar was ready for the experiment to begin. "Now we'll start adding drops of water to each jar as it if were raining," Kobe said as he measured out three equal cups of water. He slowly poured water into each of the jars, one by one. As he worked, Molly took pictures and Tomas watched carefully with pencil and notebook in hand.

By the time the experiment was over, the three were eager to share their findings with the rest of their class the next day. Tomas wrote out the results of their experiments and the conclusions they drew about what had happened in the school parking lot.

Just then, the door opened and Mrs. Hansen poked her head in. "Hey, guys, you might want to get over to the school," she said. "Your dad called and said it looks like the engineers have arrived."

Kobe, Molly, and Tomas all jumped on their bikes and headed over to the school. Several people were operating a large, loud machine next to the sinkhole.

Mr. Jennings saw them and wandered over. "I figured you would all be here," he said.

"What are they doing?" Molly asked.

"They are using the machine to take a deep sample of the dirt. This is

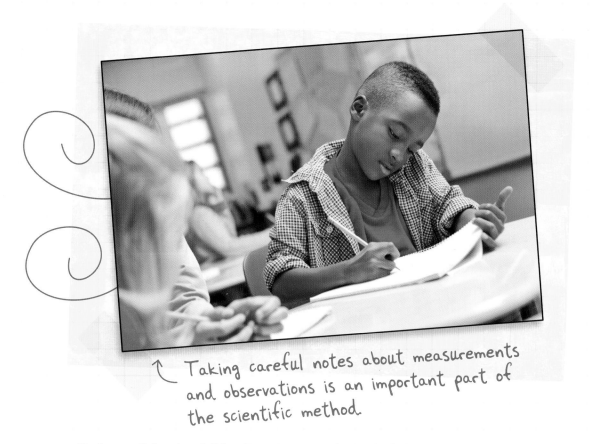

Taking careful notes about measurements and observations is an important part of the scientific method.

called a soil boring," Mr. Jennings explained. "This will give the engineers clear, specific information about the strength and consistency of the ground beneath the school. That will help the school administration figure out if there is a risk of more sinkholes forming."

"That's so cool," Kobe replied.

Mr. Jennings smiled. "It sure is. Speaking of sinkholes, are you ready to do an experiment in class tomorrow?"

"Absolutely," Tomas said. "We have notes and pictures to share with everyone."

"Fantastic! We will follow your experiment with a presentation by Ms. Matthews, the geologist," Mr. Jennings added.

"I can't believe I'm saying this, but I can't wait for school to start up again tomorrow!" Molly said, causing everyone to laugh.

TRY THIS AT HOME

This activity works best if you can find a wide variety of stones.

Water isn't the only thing that can cause rocks to erode and form sinkholes. Try out this project to see how wind can also erode rocks. The sandpaper represents years of wind blowing sand against different rocks. How does the sandpaper affect different types of rocks?

Materials Needed:
- A small piece of 50-grain sandpaper
- Several types of stones, including soft types such as limestone or dolomite as well as harder types

Directions:
1. Pick up a stone and rub it with the piece of sandpaper for 5 to 10 minutes.
2. Note what type of stone it is and how the sandpaper changes its appearance.
3. Choose a different type of stone and repeat the process. Note what effect the sandpaper has on different kinds of stones. Do you see why ground that has soft rock beneath the soil is at greater risk of being affected by sinkholes?

CHAPTER 5

TIME TO SHARE

It's important to speak clearly and explain things carefully when presenting information.

Mr. Jennings grinned at Kobe and gave him a thumbs-up. He was pleased with the experiment the three friends had shared with the class. It was clear that the students had enjoyed it—and learned from it.

"To sum it all up," Kobe said, "our experiment proved my hypothesis was correct. Water moved through the three different types of soil at different speeds. The model we used for the experiment also shows how erosion impacts the earth. Rain seeps through the topsoil and down to the soft limestone rocks underneath. Over time, the stones crack. Finally, they begin to dissolve, just like the sugar cubes did."

"When the cubes—or stones—get weak enough, the heavy, wet soil begins to sink," Molly said. "Then you get a sinkhole like the one they are fixing in our parking lot."

"Or the ones in our jars," Kobe piped in.

"Florida is known for its sinkholes because of all the limestone it has," Tomas continued. "It also gets a lot of rain during tropical storms and hurricanes. Drilling, pumping water out of the ground, and doing construction often make the situation even worse."

"Too bad the ground isn't really made of sugar cubes like in the

Major changes to land can sometimes lead to sinkholes forming.

Sinkholes can be amazing to witness, but they are also dangerous.

experiment," said one of the students. "If we had to have a sinkhole, at least it might taste good!" Everyone chuckled.

"You guys have done a great job of creating, testing, analyzing, and discussing this hypothesis," said Ms. Matthews as she walked to the front of the class. "I still remember the sinkhole at Winter Park back in 1981. In fact, visiting that huge hole when I was just a little girl was one of the main reasons I decided to become a geologist. I was fascinated by the idea that the earth could open up and swallow cars, buildings, and houses." She reached over and picked up a sugar cube. "I have to admit, though," she added, "I would prefer if there were sugar in those sinkholes." She popped the cube into her mouth and laughed along with the rest of the class.

THE BIGGEST HOLES IN THE WORLD

The 2007 Guatemala sinkhole destroyed several homes. ↳

While most sinkholes are only a few feet in diameter, some of them are huge! The biggest ones tend to be caused by human activities. They can be the result of anything from an overflowing sewer system to soil that has been contaminated with chemicals.

Off the coast of Belize is the Great Blue Hole. This circular sinkhole is 984 feet (300 m) across and 407 feet (124 m) deep. Way up on a mountainside of Venezuela is Sima Humboldt, a sinkhole that is more than 1,000 feet (305 m) deep. In 2007, a huge sinkhole appeared in Guatemala, forcing hundreds of people to evacuate the area. Three years later, another one appeared and swallowed a three-story factory. The world's largest sinkhole is found in China. Called Xiaozhai Tiankeng (Heavenly Pit), it is 2,054 feet (626 m) long, 1,762 feet (537 m) wide, and 2,172 feet (662 m) deep!

GLOSSARY

acidic (uh-SID-ik) having a sour or bitter taste

cavities (KAV-i-teez) empty spaces in something solid

cenotes (seh-NOH-teez) deep natural wells formed by the collapse of surface limestone

contaminate (kuhn-TAM-uh-nayt) add harmful or undesirable substances

dolostone (DOH-loh-stohn) rock made from the mineral dolomite

drought (DROUT) a long period without rain

erosion (i-ROH-zhuhn) the process by which something is worn away by water or wind

geologists (jee-AH-luh-jists) scientists who specialize in studying the processes and composition of the earth

hypothesis (hy-PAH-thi-sis) an idea that could explain how something works but has to be tested through experiments to be proven right

joints (JOINTS) fractures or cracks in rocks

limestone (LIME-stohn) a type of rock that is formed from the remains of shells or coral

topsoil (TAHP-soil) the usually thin top layer of soil that contains the nutrients that plants need to grow

FOR MORE INFORMATION

BOOKS

Friend, Sandra. *Sinkholes*. Sarasota, FL: Pineapple Press, 2002.

Kopp, Megan. *Sinkholes*. New York: Av2 by Weigl, 2013.

Lindop, Laurie. *Cave Sleuths*. Minneapolis: Twenty-First Century Books, 2006.

Somervill, Barbara A. *Florida*. New York: Children's Press, 2008.

WEB SITES

National Geographic: Education—Sinkhole

http://education.nationalgeographic.com/education/encyclopedia /sinkhole/?ar_a=1

Check out cool photos and learn more about sinkholes.

PBS Kids Go!—Dragonfly TV

http://pbskids.org/dragonflytv/show/sinkholes.html

Follow along with some kid explorers as they check out sinkholes in Minnesota.

TIME Explains: Sinkholes

http://content.time.com/time/video/player/0,32068,2603162825001 _2149482,00.html

Watch a brief but dramatic video about sinkholes.

INDEX

acidity, 12–13

Belize, 29

cavities, 13
cenotes, 13, 14
China, 29
cover-collapse sinkholes, 14
cover-subsidence sink-holes, 14

depths, 7, 14, 16, 29
dolostone, 10
drought, 10

erosion, 13, 25, 26

geological maps, 15
geologists, 17, 20, 28
Great Blue Hole, 29
Guatemala, 29

joints, 13

karst, 10

Lake Rose, 9
limestone, 10, 12, 13, 19, 22, 23, 25, 27

Mexico, 14

pollution, 8–9, 29
prediction, 17

rain, 9, 10, 12, 21–22, 26–27
repair, 8–9, 17
risk, 10, 15, 17, 18, 24

scientific method, 22
Sima Humboldt, 29
sizes, 7, 14, 16, 29

topsoil, 23, 26

U.S. Geological Survey, 14, 15

Venezuela, 29

warning signs, 6, 13, 18
width, 7, 16, 29
wind, 25
Winter Park, Florida, 6–8, 14, 28

Xiaozhai Tiankeng ("Heavenly Pit"), 29

Yucatan Peninsula, 14

ABOUT THE AUTHOR

Tamra Orr is an author living in the Pacific Northwest. Orr has a degree in secondary education and English from Ball State University. She is the mother of four and the author of hundreds of books for readers of all ages. When she isn't writing or reading books, she is writing letters to friends all over the world. Although fascinated by all aspects of science, most of her current scientific method skills are put to use tracking down lost socks, missing keys, and overdue library books.